The Leadership Series

Heads of War

... Volume 4

BELIAL

THE WORTHLESS ONE

WRITTEN BY

Joseph Henderson

WESTBOW
PRESS®
A DIVISION OF THOMAS NELSON
& ZONDERVAN

Illustrations and Cover designed
by Hender-Tree Publications

HenderTree Publications books may be ordered by contacting:

HenderTree Publications
P.O Box 942
Skyland, NC 28776
www.hendertree.com

-or-

WestBow Press books may be ordered through booksellers or by contacting:

WestBow Press
A Division of Thomas Nelson & Zondervan
1663 Liberty Drive
Bloomington, IN 47403
www.westbowpress.com
1 (866) 928-1240

ISBN: 978-1-9736-1281-0 (sc)
ISBN: 978-1-9736-1283-4 (hc)
ISBN: 978-1-9736-1282-7 (e)

Library of Congress Control Number: 2017919755

Print information available on the last page.

WestBow Press rev. date: 08/21/2018

Dedicated to Father GOD

Contents

A Personal Note

After many years of in-depth study, research, and training, and with the extensive insight the Holy Spirit has provided me, I can say with certainty that the information presented in these pages are accurate. This book is straightforward and offers a vast array of cold, hard facts. I can attest to some of these facts through personal experience.

Since I accepted Jesus as my Lord and Savior, I have received freedom from an oath and a blood pact I made with the kingdom of darkness. Since my conversion, I have been set free from a host of demonic possessions. GOD, by HIS mercy and grace, delivered me from the bondage of a lifestyle I was ensnared in. Among other things, this lifestyle involved performing black magic and creating and operating a satanic priesthood.

I will forever be grateful to GOD for HIS gift of salvation and for the privilege of serving in HIS kingdom of righteousness, mercy, and truth. It is my hope and prayer that you also belong to GOD'S kingdom or that you will decide to join soon, because if you choose to wait, you may find that you are too late. After all, we are not promised tomorrow on planet earth.

Introduction

This book presents a collection of mysterious information and hidden secrets. The information will serve as a guide into known and unknown worlds existing today. When addressing these various topics, many elements of the supernatural realm will be revealed. Although the subjects range from earth's creation to present and future events, they all have one thing in common: an unseen being named Belial.

This book is designed to expose this grotesque being. To accurately describe Belial, certain controversial subject matter must be examined. Various topics will be brought out of the darkness to reveal what this individual is capable of doing. Some of the subjects include violent or sexual content, so it is recommended that minors obtain approval from their parents or guardians before beginning to explore this information.

Some individuals may dismiss portions of this book as fairy tales or products of sheer imagination. Others may consider the topics to be distasteful, offensive, or lacking importance. Some may scoff at or mock these writings. But those who prayerfully ponder the information presented here have a great opportunity to gain a broader understanding of reality. A reality that may not be seen by eyes, but exist and is influencing many peoples decisions.

Not every person possesses the same belief system. However, regardless of an individual's beliefs or opinions, one fact remains: GOD'S Word is the foundation of all truth. GOD'S Word holds limitless knowledge. GOD'S Word is powerful and is contained in a book called the Holy Bible. For these reasons the majority of evidence used to prove Belial's existence comes from the King James Version of GOD'S Word.

Although GOD'S Word is the foundation and source of all truth, it is not the only resource used to reveal facts about Belial. Bits of information about this supernatural being are found in occult doctrines. And while such doctrines are dangerous and deceptive, the information gathered from these resources was carefully vetted, and used in this book for teaching purposes only.

Rest assured, GOD has always used whatever resource HE chooses to communicate truth to people. GOD can work through any channel or circumstance to get HIS message across. One example of GOD'S ability to work through whomever or whatever HE chooses can be found in the Holy Bible's Old Testament book of Numbers.

In Numbers 22:28–35, GOD wanted to get the attention of a man named Balaam. GOD chose to communicate with Balaam through Balaam's donkey, having the animal speak in a language the man understood. This proves GOD can cause animals to speak if HE deems necessary. If GOD can use an animal to speak in a human language, HE is certainly able to use any means to reveal HIS purpose.

GOD wants the truth to be known, and this is the reason HE sends prophets and teachers to reveal HIS Word. Now GOD has chosen to send forth another timely word from the spiritual realm to the physical realm. GOD'S truth and warnings are revealed throughout *The Leadership Series: Heads of War*. These supernatural revelations begin in volume four, *Belial: The Worthless One*.

In this volume is GOD'S account of creation and war. So by the command of the Creator, Father GOD (Yahweh); the authority of HIS Son, Jesus (Yeshua), and the power of GOD'S Holy Spirit, volume four of *The Leadership Series* is released to benefit humanity.

CHAPTER 1

Belial: The Beginning

"In the beginning GOD created the heavens and the earth." What a compelling statement! This powerful declaration has echoed around the world from generation to generation. These words offer countless insight and have brought to life many religious beliefs and spiritual groups. So the quest to expose a notorious being named Belial will start "in the beginning" of a story about creation.

Many explanations of creation appear in numerous forms and religious traditions. The account of creation this book will use shall come from the Holy Bible.

The Holy Bible is one large book containing sixty-six smaller books. These books were penned by various writers. Each received inspiration and guidance from our Creator and put the Almighty's revelations into words.

Genesis, the first book of the Holy Bible, explains how the heavens, the earth, and Belial came into existence. While its authorship is debated, most believe Genesis was written by a historical leader named Moses. In this book Moses put into words the revelations GOD gave him regarding phenomenal events that had taken place before the creation of humanity. These enlightening words begin with chapter 1, verse 1, and read as follows:

"In the beginning God created the heaven and the earth."

This first verse tells how the heavens and the earth were formed. The phrase "God created" shows that a supernatural entity established the heavens and the earth. However, verse 2 of the same chapter suggests that something changed. Verse 2 reads as follows:

"And the earth was without form, and void; and darkness was upon the face of the deep. And the Spirit of God moved upon the face of the waters."

Verse 2 presents a different view of earth than verse 1 does. Verse 1 states "God created" (or formed) the heavens and planet earth. However, verse 2 states the earth was "without form, and void." This revelation raises an interesting question. What could have transpired to reduce the perfect creation of verse 1 to a formless wasteland?

The answer can be found by exploring an unknown era between the two verses—a time when powerful beings freely roamed the cosmos. To show how the transformation came about and to further explain this period between verses 1 and 2, a short story is offered.

The Beginning

GOD brought into existence the heavens and the beginning of time. The Almighty spoke with explosive power, and some of the first life forms in the cosmos were brought into being.

These pioneering entities were given the task of serving GOD and completing HIS will. The newly formed individuals were only the first of many creations the Almighty had planned for the vast realms of the cosmos. Some of these first spiritual beings were called Archons.

GOD continued to bring about all HE willed. The heavens developed rapidly because the Creator made vast legions of supernatural beings to serve and build at HIS discretion. Archon, angelic, and all other spiritual beings focused on their assigned tasks.

Inch by inch and mile by mile, the heavens and the universes were constructed according to GOD'S plan. A wide array of realms and dimensions continuously came into being as creation unfolded for all to bear witness.

And bear witness all did to the glory of their Creator. GOD'S designs generated such splendor that all those who beheld it praised HIS holy name.

As he moved about in the heavens, one of GOD'S angels intently observed all of his master's doings. However, this attentiveness was not fueled by a passion to lift up a holy and benevolent GOD. On the contrary, this individual was completely focused on something else.

This angelic being gazed at the inhabitants of the

cosmos praising and adoring GOD their Creator. He was entranced by this worship. The angel's name was Lucifer.

As time passed and he kept observing all the praise given to GOD, an unholy desire arose in this servant of the Almighty. With his passions growing, Lucifer's perspective changed. Now, instead of seeking to serve GOD, he looked to exalt himself.

Lucifer embellished on his own gifts and abilities, and when the urge for admiration had completely overtaken him, his loyalties changed. Now the angel of GOD wanted to experience glory for himself. Lucifer longed to have what belonged to GOD. This angel wanted to do what GOD did and to be exalted as GOD was.

With this unholy obsession drawing him, Lucifer fantasized what it would be like to be as GOD. One small fantasy grew into another and another. Before long, his imagination drove the angel to contemplate a more concrete idea. He would secretly seek out someone who would admire him and would sing his praises in the universe.

Earth

As Lucifer harbored these idolatrous thoughts, GOD, the Almighty, and Initiator of new things, continued to fill the heavenly realms with solar systems and their inhabitants. It was time for the hand of GOD to turn towards the planet we human beings call earth.

GOD formed this planet's atmosphere to support life. Earth's creatures would be able to crawl, run, and climb. Some species would possess the ability to fly and to swim.

With the earth's atmosphere and environment completed, GOD began creating this vast array of species to dwell on the planet. As HE did so, HE established how the earthly realm would function.

Every being was assigned specific duties. And although these life forms were of varying sizes and shapes and occupied different domains, harmony reigned because the Creator had ordained peace on the planet.

As GOD completed this stage of creation, one species could be seen living beside another in accord. In the beginning all these entities did what they were supposed to do, fulfilling the purpose for which they had been created.

GOD saw what HE had accomplished and was satisfied. HE knew this would not be the end of HIS work on the planet but just the beginning of what the entire cosmos would see HIM do.

GOD moved on to other projects in the heavens. As the focus of the universe turned to places other than the third planet from the sun, questions began to form. Could the earth stay the way GOD commanded it to be, or could a change be coming soon? Would something in the cosmos want to alter GOD'S order?

Belial

Lucifer saw GOD'S work on earth and its ongoing progress. Again living beings were created at GOD'S command, and the Creator received more praise throughout the cosmos.

This continuing praise further fueled the angel's growing envy. He was determined even more to gain adoration for himself and kept looking for a way to make this happen.

Then something caught his attention. For a moment, the angel's thoughts were diverted from himself to another. He became aware of an Archon who seemed to isolate himself from others whenever possible.

Intrigued, Lucifer covertly observed the Archon at every opportunity. The angel quickly learned of this individual's growing reputation for persuasive powers.

This Archon managed to live a comfortable life at the expense of others. He had an ability to get someone else to tend to his responsibilities and to do what he wanted. His name was Belial.

At first the angel took a dim view of Belial, wondering how it was possible for a creature with such incredible abilities to conduct himself like this. But then he paused. It was obvious to Lucifer that Belial's loyalties lay with himself. Knowing this individual's operating style might prove beneficial to Lucifer's plan.

So Lucifer arranged a private meeting with the Archon. When the two met, the angel began the conversation with tactful words, seeking to make a lasting impression on Belial.

The atmosphere remained casual until the conversation turned to self-willed independence. When that topic arose, Belial showed more enthusiasm. The Archon spoke of the times he had fantasized about living without having to be accountable to anyone.

When Lucifer heard this, he knew he had found what he was looking for. Belial's independent spirit gave Lucifer the opportunity he needed for his plan to work.

Right away the angel began to entice Belial by offering him a false independence. Lucifer bombarded the Archon with promises of grandeur. He used crafty words to reinforce Belial's belief that there was nothing wrong with rejecting GOD'S authority and with wanting to be self-ruled. Lucifer insinuated that Belial could live as the mighty angel had chosen, in service to self.

Belial was momentarily awed at that thought and then shouted praises to Lucifer and his new ideology. The angel relished every moment of glory he had coerced, but Belial's praise was not enough to satisfy Lucifer's ever-expanding ego.

With this taste of acknowledgment, the angel wanted more recognition, more praise, and more worship. Lucifer had talked himself into believing the promises of grandeur he had impressed upon Belial. This angelic being saw himself as unaccountable to anyone and believed himself greater than all. But what was Lucifer willing to do to fulfill these new desires, and how could he make them a reality?

The Rebellion Begins

Urged on by support from Belial, Lucifer was filled with fiendish thoughts. Should he settle for a little praise behind the scenes, or did he feel he deserved to be praised openly by all creation?

With his soaring ego, Lucifer did not think being hidden away and revered by a select few would be enough honor. Belial agreed. This was all the encouragement the crafty angel needed to convince himself he deserved adulation from the multitudes.

Belial reservedly asked Lucifer about GOD, and the angel paused for a moment. Lucifer realized if he tried to steal praise and worship from GOD, the attempt would not go unnoticed. Lucifer knew that GOD would not tolerate such treachery and that the Almighty's judgment would be swift and severe.

Lucifer answered that he and those allies he might gather could not stand against GOD'S entire force. After a brief silence, Belial posed a question to Lucifer. If a portion of heaven's army could somehow be neutralized, would there be a chance for their plan to succeed?

Lucifer knew there was no possibility of neutralizing the entire heavenly host, but he did have an idea. The angel imagined if he made the right moves, it might be possible to control portions of the cosmos. And if he could gain control over realms of the universe, why wouldn't it be possible for him to control portions of GOD'S capital, the celestial city?

This idea carried great risks. After all, no one had ever made such a move before. But Lucifer knew that even if his idea proved only half successful, he would be sure to receive all the acknowledgment he craved.

The angel's desire to be worshipped caused his life to spin completely out of control. Lucifer's fantasies had been transformed into an attempt to topple GOD'S authority. Now there was no turning back.

Lucifer quickly enlisted Belial's service. The Archon felt overjoyed at being asked to help in such an undertaking. The two became relentless in their scheme to overthrow GOD'S order.

Their first objective was to begin secretly mesmerizing those heavenly beings who were in positions of authority. Lucifer knew that for his plan to work, he must somehow turn various species against their Creator. The angel also knew this sabotage would have to be accomplished without initially attracting too much attention.

So creating dissension became the focus for Lucifer and Belial. The two beings cleverly wove webs of trickery and illusion. The angel and the Archon were willing to do anything to gain self-rule and independence from their Creator.

A New Kingdom

Their momentum was slow in the beginning. Only a small number of cosmic inhabitants were convinced to join the rebellion. Gaining support for this overthrow attempt proved difficult because the vast majority of GOD'S creation loved and revered HIM.

Lucifer met with those loyal to him and gave them new instructions. These followers were now commissioned to use any deception, bribery, or torturous act they deemed necessary to bring an army of species under the angel's rule. Lucifer knew he must enlist a vast number of cosmic inhabitants without delay, or the revolt's element of surprise could be threatened.

Belial submitted a clever idea to his boss. These rebels needed to convince a mass population that they were not rebelling against GOD but that a new kingdom was developing under the old. This strategy might make it easier to gain support, and once the truth came out, it would be too late. Lucifer approved of Belial's idea, and the rebellion was given a new appearance.

The change would prove useful. With the rebellion's new appearance, Lucifer could become the icon of a new and free kingdom, one that condoned intoxicating pleasures and approved of forbidden desires. This new kingdom would be led by Lucifer and those he delegated to represent his interests.

The leadership offices in this new kingdom were reserved for those who pledged their loyalty to Lucifer and to the new order. Despicable individuals who practiced acts of wickedness could easily advance in the selection process. Immediately under the angel were three leadership positions carrying the title of crown prince. However, along with the title and the prestige came a tremendous amount of responsibility to Lucifer.

Because the Archons had proved to be among the most powerful species, Lucifer needed their cooperation to subdue a vast array of heavenly entities. He needed to gain an undeniable influence with the Archon species and to prove it with some type of public declaration. So Lucifer decided it was good politics to select an Archon as the first crown prince in his kingdom. And he had the perfect Archon in mind: Belial.

Belial was chosen because he had proven himself loyal and had done everything expected of him. No matter how detestable or challenging the assignment was, Belial demonstrated the ability to get the job done. Even though this Archon was greedy and self-centered, Lucifer showed no concern. Lucifer knew Belial feared what would happen to him if he double-crossed the angel.

Lucifer summoned Belial and informed him of his new position. The angel had arranged for an inauguration ceremony to take place immediately. During the ceremony, the initiate would take an oath and swear allegiance to Lucifer.

Belial participated in this demonic ceremony and eagerly took the oath of office, pledging his life to a new master and god: Lucifer. As the ceremony concluded, the angel embraced Belial with a cold touch of death and allowed the Archon a vision of who he would become in the new kingdom.

From that moment on, Belial served the rebel kingdom with more zeal, using persuasion, bribery, and violence. He would do anything to please Lucifer. With his enhanced supernatural abilities, Belial relentlessly promoted the rising kingdom and gathered a large force in no time. As Belial grew in strength, so did Lucifer and the rebellion.

Soon Lucifer selected the other two crown princes, and they were sworn into office. Now a shift of power could be felt in different realms and dimensions. For one reason or another, a variety of cosmic inhabitants joined the new kingdom. There was still resistance in key places, but all those targeted by Lucifer but reluctant to join him were quickly subdued and forced into slave labor for the new regime. The first phase of the rebellion was proceeding according to plan, as most of the individuals needed to amass a formidable force were enlisted or enslaved by the emerging kingdom.

The earth was invaded and fell under the influence of the rebel kingdom. A planet marked by harmony and peace descended into violence and bloodshed. The earth's creatures rebelled against GOD'S order and attacked each other. Where life once thrived, death now prevailed.

With the help of Belial and others, Lucifer brought chaos to the earth and other realms. Destruction was widespread. And as portions of the universe began to unravel and war in the heavens seemed unavoidable, lines would soon be drawn in the sand.

Having seized many realms, including earth, the rebel leaders shifted their focus to the next phase of the plan. They were aware that when their soldiers invaded the celestial city, they would need support from within heaven's army. For this reason Lucifer and his agents had already persuaded, bribed, or disillusioned certain angels enlisted in the heavenly ranks.

Now that Lucifer had demonstrated his intent to bring about a new order, many of these wooed and enticed angels became intrigued with the ideology of the new empire. The offers of power and prestige consumed the thoughts of some in the angelic ranks to the degree that many pledged their loyalty to Lucifer.

When the agreements were finalized, Lucifer had gained the full cooperation of a sizable angelic force. These angels were ordered to remain inconspicuous in and around the celestial city and to wait until the rebel army reached the city before joining the fight. When the rebels invaded, these traitorous angels would be positioned in strategic locations to reinforce the mutineers' attempt to overthrow GOD'S order.

The War at Hand

The outbreak of war was obvious as the rebel forces marched on the plains toward GOD'S celestial city.

Leading the invasion was Lucifer, who was now an angel of war.

As Lucifer's enormous force approached the outskirts of the celestial city, fierce battles erupted everywhere between the angels of GOD and the rebels. These battles became brutal. They were so intense that the heavens shook. Then as fast as a strike of lightning hitting the ground, the ferocious fight was over.

GOD had seen enough and crushed the invasion. The rebel army was quickly defeated, and Lucifer stood helpless and beaten. Shame and disgrace fell upon those who had chosen to rebel against their Creator. Even the crafty Belial was speechless.

Without hesitation, GOD pronounced judgment upon all the sinful and rebellious creatures. HE put some of the judgments into action immediately but delayed the implementation of others. As the entire universe witnessed the execution of these punishments upon the traitors, GOD demonstrated to HIS creation that HE was and always would be supreme.

Lucifer and the other rebels were hastily removed from GOD'S presence. The rebel force was cast out of the third heaven and was hurled toward earth. The planet, with its newly restructured atmosphere, became a prison where these rebels would be held until their judgments were completed.

The Truth Revealed

Now one can perceive how GOD'S perfect earth was reduced to a formless wasteland. The Holy Bible makes several references to this battle in the heavens. One reference is found in the Old Testament book of Isaiah 14:12–17. The passage reads as follows:

12. How art thou fallen from heaven, O Lucifer, son of the morning! how art thou cut down to the ground, which didst weaken the nations!

13. For thou hast said in thine heart, I will ascend into heaven, I will exalt my throne above the stars of God: I will sit also upon the mount of the congregation, in the sides of the north:

14. I will ascend above the heights of the clouds; I will be like the most High.

15. Yet thou shalt be brought down to hell, to the sides of the pit.

16. They that see thee shall narrowly look upon thee, and consider thee, saying, Is this the man that made the earth to tremble, that did shake kingdoms;

17. That made the world as a wilderness, and destroyed the cities thereof; that opened not the house of his prisoners?

These verses provide valuable insight into how Lucifer, Belial, and the rebel forces fell from grace. Verse 12 shows where Lucifer and those who supported him had "fallen," or were thrown "from heaven." This verse reveals that Lucifer and those who served him were sentenced to earth, or "cut down to the ground." Verse 12 also mentions Lucifer "didst weaken the nations," corrupting earth's inhabitants with his influences.

Verses 13 and 14 reveal motives for the rebellion. Lucifer and his conspirators wanted to be like the Almighty, so they attempted to overthrow GOD'S order. These two verses also provide a list of crimes committed by this fallen angel and his defeated army.

Verses 15 and 16 reveal more judgments placed upon Lucifer and his followers, saying these rebels were "brought down to hell."

Verse 17 makes two interesting points. First, this verse proves that Lucifer's rebellious war brought severe judgment upon this world. When GOD created the earth, it was beautiful and alive, but Lucifer's rebellion made "the world as a wilderness."

The second point to note was what transpired for earth's inhabitants. Before the rebellion, advanced populations had built cities large and small. However, because earth's inhabitants chose to rebel against GOD'S divine order and to serve Lucifer, everyone and everything on the planet suffered (severe punishment and retribution) for their sinful disobedience and ultimately "destroyed the cities thereof."

GOD had intended for creation to be productive and prosperous, but Lucifer's plans brought loss and shame to himself and to many cosmic inhabitants. GOD initiated harmony and order, but Lucifer brought pain and suffering to those who followed him. These judgments were only the beginning. More judgments will be implemented on these rebels for their treacherous actions.

So be conscious of the fact that somewhere on the earth fallen beings await further punishment by GOD. Be aware of the fact that Lucifer, Belial, and the rebel hosts have been imprisoned here on earth for a long time and still reside among us. Remember that a war was waged in the heavens but has now transitioned to earth.

However, the objective of the war has changed. The war began with an attempt to overthrow GOD'S heavenly order, and that attempt proved unsuccessful. Now the rebel army's objective is to overthrow GOD'S order on earth and to destroy the souls of mankind.

CHAPTER 2

What GOD Said Regarding Belial

The Holy Bible contains numerous references to Belial. He is mentioned in Old and New Testament books. Some passages refer to Belial by name, while others merely discuss his characteristics.

Provided in this chapter is a biblical reference guide listing a variety of passages pertaining to Belial. Although this guide contains many references, it is not conclusive, so feel free to explore GOD'S Word to learn more about what the Creator of the universe has revealed concerning Belial.

Reference Guide

Deuteronomy	13:13
Judges	19:22
Judges	20:13
I Samuel	1:16
I Samuel	2:12
I Samuel	10:27
I Samuel	25:17, 25

I Samuel	30:22
II Samuel	16:7
II Samuel	20:1
II Samuel	23:6
I Kings	21:10, 13
II Chronicles	13:7
II Corinthians	6:15

The First Illustration

Examined in this chapter are two illustrations found in the Old Testament. The first is located in Deuteronomy 13:12–18. (The book of Deuteronomy is also part of the Torah.) The passage reads as follows:

12. **If thou shalt hear say in one of thy cities, which the LORD thy God hath given thee to dwell there, saying,**

13. **Certain men, the children of Belial, are gone out from among you, and have withdrawn the inhabitants of their city, saying, Let us go and serve other gods, which ye have not known;**

14.**Then shalt thou enquire, and make search, and ask diligently; and, behold, if it be truth, and the thing certain, that such abomination is wrought among you;**

15. **Thou shalt surely smite the inhabitants of that city with the edge of the sword, destroying it utterly, and all that is therein, and the cattle thereof, with the edge of the sword.**

16. **And thou shalt gather all the spoil of it into the midst of the street thereof, and shalt burn with fire the city, and all the spoil thereof every whit, for the LORD thy God: and it shall be an heap for ever; it shall not be built again.**

17. **And there shall cleave nought of the cursed thing to thine hand: that the LORD may turn from the fierceness of his anger, and shew thee mercy, and have compassion upon thee, and multiply thee, as he hath sworn unto thy fathers;**

18. **When thou shalt hearken to the voice of the LORD thy God, to keep all his commandments which I command thee this day, to do that which is right in the eyes of the LORD thy God.**

This passage contains words of passion, words of vigilance, and words of judgment. In verse 12 Moses warns leaders to pay attention to what they hear in their jurisdictions and to what is being reported in their cities.

In verse 13, when Moses mentions "Certain men, the children of Belial," he is referring to individuals who follow and serve this leader of the dark kingdom. Moses also points out that the goals of these "children of Belial" are to persuade "the inhabitants of their city, saying, Let us go and serve other gods, which ye have not known."

In verse 14 Moses issues a decree to those in authority. They must "enquire, and make search, and ask diligently" about any accusation or suspicions. In other words, those in charge of an area where allegations surface are to investigate any legitimate report and to verify if demonic activities are occurring. These leaders must be thorough in every investigation because the truth must be found out.

Verse 15 makes clear what is to be done to those who willfully commit spiritual treason and align themselves with the enemies of humanity. If "inhabitants of that city" are found guilty of such treachery, they are to be slain "with the edge of the sword."

However, judgment does not end with the death of the guilty. Verse 16 says all the belongings of the traitors are to be taken "into the midst of the street" and burned "with fire" never to "be built again."

The remaining two verses present words of caution and words of blessing. In verse 17 Moses warns people not to keep anything belonging to those who followed Belial. They are to "cleave nought of the cursed thing to thine hand." In verse 18 he advises people it is wise to listen to GOD and obey HIM—to "hearken to the voice of the LORD thy God, to keep all his commandments."

Verses 17 and 18 also declare blessings for obedience. In verse 17 Moses says "the LORD may turn from the fierceness of his anger, and shew thee mercy, and have compassion upon thee, and multiply thee, as he hath sworn unto thy fathers." In verse 18 Moses tells GOD'S people how they may always be blessed. Blessings will always follow those who "do that which is right in the eyes of the LORD thy God."

The Second Illustration

A second illustration of how GOD'S Word exposes Belial comes from the Old Testament book of Judges, chapter 19 in its entirety.

This chapter has sexual and violent content. Because of the nature of the material, parents must decide whether to introduce such topics to their minor children. The chapter reads as follows:

1. And it came to pass in those days, when there was no king in Israel, that there was a certain Levite sojourning on the side of mount Ephraim, who took to him a concubine out of Beth-lehem-judah.

2. And his concubine played the whore against him, and went away from him unto her father's house to Beth-lehem-judah, and was there four whole months.

3. And her husband arose, and went after her, to speak friendly unto her, and to bring her again, having his servant with him, and a couple of asses: and she brought him into her father's house: and when

the father of the damsel saw him, he rejoiced to meet him.

4. And his father in law, the damsel's father, retained him; and he abode with him three days: so they did eat and drink, and lodged there.

5. And it came to pass on the fourth day, when they arose early in the morning, that he rose up to depart: and the damsel's father said unto his son in law, Comfort thine heart with a morsel of bread, and afterward go your way.

6. And they sat down, and did eat and drink both of them together: for the damsel's father had said unto the man, Be content, I pray thee, and tarry all night, and let thine heart be merry.

7. And when the man rose up to depart, his father in law urged him: therefore he lodged there again.

8. And he arose early in the morning on the fifth day to depart: and the damsel's father said, Comfort thine heart, I pray thee. And they tarried until afternoon, and they did eat both of them.

9. And when the man rose up to depart, he, and his concubine, and his servant, his father in law, the damsel's father, said unto him, Behold, now the day draweth toward evening, I pray you tarry all night:

behold, the day groweth to an end, lodge here, that thine heart may be merry; and to morrow get you early on your way, that thou mayest go home.

10. But the man would not tarry that night, but he rose up and departed, and came over against Jebus, which is Jerusalem; and there were with him two asses saddled, his concubine also was with him.

11. And when they were by Jebus, the day was far spent; and the servant said unto his master, Come, I pray thee, and let us turn in into this city of the Jebusites, and lodge in it.

12. And his master said unto him, We will not turn aside hither into the city of a stranger, that is not of the children of Israel; we will pass over to Gibeah.

13. And he said unto his servant, Come, and let us draw near to one of these places to lodge all night, in Gibeah, or in Ramah.

14. And they passed on and went their way; and the sun went down upon them when they were by Gibeah, which belongeth to Benjamin.

15. And they turned aside thither, to go in and to lodge in Gibeah: and when he went in, he sat him down in a street of the city: for there was no man that took them into his house to lodging.

16. And, behold, there came an old man from his work out of the field at even, which was also of mount Ephraim; and he sojourned in Gibeah: but the men of the place were Benjamites.

17. And when he had lifted up his eyes, he saw a wayfaring man in the street of the city: and the old man said, Whither goest thou? and whence comest thou?

18. And he said unto him, We are passing from Beth-lehem-judah toward the side of mount Ephraim; from thence am I: and I went to Beth-lehem-judah, but I am now going to the house of the LORD; and there is no man that receiveth me to house.

19. Yet there is both straw and provender for our asses; and there is bread and wine also for me, and for thy hand-maid, and for the young man which is with thy servants: there is no want of any thing.

20. And the old man said, Peace be with thee; howsoever let all thy wants lie upon me; only lodge not in the street.

21. So he brought him into his house, and gave provender unto the asses: and they washed their feet, and did eat and drink.

22. Now as they were making their hearts merry, behold, the men of the city, certain sons of Belial, beset the house round about, and beat at the door, and spake to the master of the house, the old man, saying, Bring forth the man that came into thine house, that we may know him.

23. And the man, the master of the house, went out unto them, and said unto them, Nay, my brethren, nay, I pray you, do not so wickedly; seeing that this man is come into mine house, do not this folly.

24. Behold, here is my daughter a maiden, and his concubine; them I will bring out now, and humble ye them, and do with them what seemeth good unto you: but unto this man do not so vile a thing.

25. But the men would not hearken to him: so the man took his concubine, and brought her forth unto them; and they knew her, and abused her all the night until the morning: and when the day began to spring, they let her go.

26. Then came the woman in the dawning of the day, and fell down at the door of the man's house where her lord was, till it was light.

27. And her lord rose up in the morning, and opened the doors of the house, and went out to go his way: and, behold, the woman his concubine was fallen

down at the door of the house, and her hands were upon the threshold.

28. And he said unto her, Up, and let us be going. But none answered. Then the man took her up upon an ass, and the man rose up, and gat him unto his place.

29. And when he was come into his house, he took a knife, and laid hold on his concubine, and divided her, together with her bones, into twelve pieces, and sent her into all the coast of Israel.

30. And it was so, that all that saw it said, There was no such deed done nor seen from the day that the children of Israel came up out of the land of Egypt unto this day: consider of it, take advice, and speak your minds.

What a painful and heart-wrenching account! The story clearly demonstrates the destruction Belial brings about once he gains access to people's lives.

In this example Belial received permission to enter the Levite's home. He was allowed access when a woman of the house embraced the enticements of this crown prince and "played the whore," as seen in verse 2. And although her sinful failure was damaging enough on its own, this was only the beginning of sorrow for the family.

This Levite family became vulnerable, according to verse 15. At the perfect time, Belial seized his opportunity and instigated a mob of his followers (v. 22). The demonically charged crowd had one goal in mind, and that was to sexually assault the Levite, a servant of GOD.

When the mob failed to secure GOD'S servant, the crown prince called for "the men of the city, certain sons of Belial," to take the Levite's concubine captive. These dastardly followers of Belial took this poor woman and repeatedly raped and assaulted her throughout the night.

The servants of Belial did their master's bidding and shattered the Levite family. Because of the unimaginable abuse inflicted upon the woman, she died. What anguish and suffering this woman and her family experienced at the hands of Belial!

CHAPTER 3

The Realms of Belial

This chapter will examine some of the realms which Belial presides over. These realms can be accessed through well-hidden entrances that operate as demonic portals or supernatural gateways.

To some, the idea of a mystic doorway from one dimension to another may seem farfetched or appear to be something that could happen only in the distant future. However, gateways have been strategically positioned throughout the world for one purpose: to bring as many people as possible onto the twisted paths leading to the destructive and deadly realms of Belial.

A Fragmented Truth

To offer insight into how certain realms of this crown prince function, some dangerous information must be shared. Also, certain cautions are advised when venturing into any area where Belial or one of his minions presides.

Caution is necessary because some of the information in this chapter was derived from occult ideology. And although many find occultism controversial, this information will add valuable insight regarding the realms of Belial.

The occult ideologies mentioned in this chapter are not recommended for reading or study. Occultism is demonically influenced and is designed to be cunning, alluring, and deceiving. Occult books, objects, or propaganda can carry an array of curses. These cursed items may have wicked spirits attached or assigned to them. If you have occult items in your home, you would be wise to dispose of them for your safety and for the safety of others.

Occult ideologies have deceived many people by using what is known as fragmented truths. A fragmented truth is a fact included in a deception to make it appear plausible. Keep in mind that an occult teaching does not become accurate just because it contains an element of truth.

Here is an example. Certain occult sects acknowledge Jesus as the Son of GOD. Adherents believe Jesus came to earth in a physical form and had a ministry here two thousand years ago. These occultists also believe Jesus died on a cross. However, they transform these truths into fragmented truths when they make them part of a doctrine that denies the resurrection of Jesus.

This doctrine not only denies the physical resurrection but offers a fabricated version of what happened after Jesus was crucified. These occultists go beyond claiming He did not rise from the grave. Their false ideology builds a foundation for further lies.

The occultists profess that after Jesus died on the cross, He was imprisoned deep within the dark pits of hell's kingdom. This is one of the reasons occult ideologies are so dangerous. Beliefs such as this deny biblical truth.

Occultists who promote this doctrine try to convince people of its accuracy by using creditable truths. It is true that Jesus is the Son of GOD. It is true that Jesus came to earth and ministered to people. It is true that Jesus gave His life on a cross. But these facts become fragmented truths when employed in an ideology claiming Jesus is dead and imprisoned in hell.

When committed followers of darkness mention Jesus, they often omit legitimate accounts of His resurrection. These servants of the rebel kingdom want to hide proof that Jesus rose from the dead, because they know this information will mean their eventual defeat. These people of darkness will not admit there is proof that days after Jesus was crucified and buried, He was seen by more than five hundred witnesses.

The proof of Jesus' resurrection after His crucifixion and burial is in GOD'S Word, the Holy Bible. Evidence of Jesus returning from the dead was recorded in the New Testament book of 1 Corinthians 15:4–8. The passage reads as follows:

4. And that he was buried, and that he rose again the third day according to the scriptures:

5. And that he was seen of Cephas, then of the twelve:

6. After that, he was seen of above five hundred brethren at once; of whom the greater part remain unto this present, but some are fallen asleep.

7. After that, he was seen of James; then of all the apostles.

8. And last of all he was seen of me also, as of one born out of due time.

That occultists deliberately ignore this proof of Jesus' resurrection demonstrates how they attempt to manipulate people's minds by using fragments of the truth. A partial truth does not make an entire statement accurate. So it's important to remember that the occult material mentioned in this chapter is extracted from among many deceptions.

This occult material comes from *The Satanic Bible*, published in 1969. The book was written by Mr. Anton LeVay, a high priest of Satan. *The Satanic Bible* consists of five smaller books. Four have their own titles. One is titled *Belial*.

Most of the smaller books are assigned a specific element. These elements play an important role because specific elements are required to access different areas of operation in the rebel kingdom. Seasoned occultists are trained to manipulate these elements. Properly manipulated elements can form keys that unlock supernatural doorways between the physical and the spiritual realms. The elemental key used to access Belial's realm is earth (or worldliness).

A geographic location accompanies each name and element. Each book gives specific instructions as to what bearing an individual must take and which element must be used to access a particular realm in the rebel kingdom. The direction of Belial's region is north. A chart will follow to simplify this explanation.

Province		Elemental Key		Direction
Belial	key of	Earth	access point	North
		(Worldliness)		

This chart clearly shows which elemental key and direction lead to the realms of Belial. He is positioned in the northern realms of the rebel kingdom, while he operates in the earthly, or worldly, element. Thus Belial wages war against humanity from his command post in the northern hemisphere of hell.

Mr. LaVey was very aware of Belial's location. He was an avid follower of Belial and of the rebel kingdom, and a devoted servant always knows where to find their master.

Although stationed in the northern provinces, Belial and his servants are not limited to attacking humanity from the north. These wicked agents can travel to any location to participate in joint operations.

Rank or territory becomes irrelevant when demons are commanded to comply with Lucifer's will. Any member of the rebel kingdom who does not submit to Lucifer's will are coerced by larger and more powerful spirits. No mercy is granted by Lucifer. No mercy is granted by any leader in the rebel kingdom, including Belial.

Pornography

Belial's objective is to ensnare as many people as possible through the vast realms he controls. One of his most successful areas of operation is the realm of pornography. (The word *pornography* originally referred only to prostitutes and prostitution, but its meaning has expanded to include sexual acts and explicit material.) Belial and his minions make skillful use of pornography, prostitution, and indecent sexual acts in their relentless war on humanity.

Belial has observed human nature since the time of Adam and Eve. He understands every human is created with a certain amount of passion and sexual desire.

GOD placed these yearnings in our DNA for a multitude of reasons. The desire to procreate enables our race to continue to exist. Sexual desire also allows a man and a woman to become one with sharing a unique intimacy and special bond.

Having insight into male and female sexuality, Belial makes every effort to corrupt the gift GOD has given to humanity. He works continuously to distort and to pervert GOD'S directive for sex.

Belial's efforts in this arena often begin by exposing the masses to suggestive materials. This crown prince uses a variety of media to bombard people's minds. Books, movies, television, and the Internet are just a few of the tools Belial uses to advertise his perverse view of sex.

If Belial can persuade a person to view pornographic material, a doorway will be established for demonic spirits. Once Belial or his minions have gained this access to someone's life, the victim will begin experiencing an influx of twisted or perverse thoughts about sex.

These thoughts are intended to affect a person's emotions, mentality, and will. Once Belial has infiltrated one of these areas, the other two will eventually fall under his influence. This crown prince realizes that when he can bring someone's mind, will, and emotions into submission, he will have gained control of the person's immortal soul.

To illustrate how Belial uses pornography to destroy lives, a short story will follow.

Frank and Shelia fell in love and married. As their new union grew, it was quite obvious to everyone who knew them that Frank and Shelia were deeply in love. Their marriage looked like a success. The couple had such a strong longing for one another that they spent every moment they could together.

One night after Frank had arrived home from work, he mentioned to Shelia that Bill, one of his coworkers, had invited them to attend a special event in three weeks. Frank said there would be no cost because the event would be held at Bill's church. After discussing it, Frank and Shelia decided it might be fun to go.

The next day Frank accepted the invitation. As the days passed, Frank interacted more frequently with Christian coworkers and was pulled away from others in the office who usually conducted themselves inappropriately. As Frank began listening to stories about Jesus, an agent of Belial noticed Frank's growing interest in the man from Galilee.

Belial learned of Frank's plan to attend the church event and of his interest in Jesus. The crown prince realized something must be done right away to detour Frank and Shelia from their upcoming commitment. He knew if they were allowed to visit this church, there was a chance Frank and Shelia could start going regularly. He knew if they began to go to church they would hear about the Son of GOD. One thing might lead to another, and they could end up giving their hearts and lives to Jesus. Belial was not going to let them slip from his evil clutches.

The Archon immediately dispatched his minions because there was only a short time before the church event. His invisible agents began to take every opportunity to whisper accusations about one another into Frank and Shelia's ears.

Eventually the whispers had their effect as the couple's simple disagreements became full-fledged arguments. With Belial's minions fanning the flames, the arguments rapidly became more frequent and intense. The couple's relationship deteriorated to the point where Frank and

Shelia refused to go anywhere together, including the church event.

When Frank told Bill what had happened, Bill tried to reach out to him, but Frank shunned his help. Belial had prevented Frank and Shelia from attending the church event, but the crown prince wasn't finished with the couple.

Strife filled Frank and Shelia's home as two lovebirds became birds of prey. The friction between the two had escalated to the point where they could not be in the same room together for five minutes without a conflict arising. Belial was achieving his goal to divide Frank and Shelia. Sadly, a man and a woman who once had such passion for each other were now drifting apart.

Shelia, a highly relational person, began feeling lonely because of the strain between her and Frank. She had always enjoyed books, so she began to read sensual novels to fill the romantic void she felt. When Shelia opened her mind and heart to these novels, Belial's agents subtly encouraged her to consider what was missing in her relationship with Frank.

When the excitement of the love novels no longer filled the void she was experiencing, Shelia decided to take some advice she had received from her sister. Her sister had suggested Shelia place an ad with an online social network. Because she was married, Shelia had resisted this idea at first. But the division between her and Frank made Shelia rethink that decision.

So Shelia chose to post an ad on a dating website. She believed no harm had been done, but she was wrong.

When Shelia placed the ad, she unknowingly opened a doorway for Belial to enter further into her life.

While Shelia mistakenly made herself vulnerable to Belial, Frank began to experience unusual happenings of his own. Agents of the crown prince bombarded Frank's mind with deceitful thoughts. These fiends first tried to convince him that Shelia was changing for the worse. They repeatedly reminded Frank that Shelia wasn't kind to him anymore. Then came the lies that she had lost interest in him and in anything he did.

As Shelia's love for Frank was effectively challenged, something within his soul started to change. For the first time, Frank began to question if he had made a mistake in marrying Shelia.

Frank felt alone and missed the passion and the intimacy he once had in his marriage. He didn't want to cheat on his wife, but the loneliness seemed to overwhelm him. Belial's agents continually whispered accusatory words in his ears, causing a downward cycle in his thought process.

Then these agents tried to convince Frank that he could ease his loneliness by secretly viewing pornography. No harm would be done to anyone, these voices suggested. These same voices told him that he could easily view pornography on the Internet and that this way no one would ever find out. Belial's agents made a convincing case, and Frank decided to turn to pornography.

Frank mentally and emotionally felt a brief distraction from his loneliness after his first viewing of Internet porn, but found nothing that completely fulfilled him. However, even with so many things missing, Frank's passions drove him to try pornography again.

One viewing led to another. Then Frank began to watch Internet porn whenever possible, hoping each time it would somehow fill his emptiness. But Frank always walked away from the screen disappointed. Internet porn could not fulfill his desires as he had hoped. All pornography did was make Frank more vulnerable to Belial's traps.

One day Frank decided what he was doing wasn't working. A fantasy that could be experienced only through a computer screen was not for him. Frank no longer wanted to sneak around on the Internet. He desired a physical relationship with a breathing human being.

At this vulnerable moment, an agent of Belial whispered something into Frank's ear. These words got his attention immediately. Frank was reminded of another relationship he already had.

Frank recalled that while at work he continually interacted with his secretary, Patty. She seemed to be a kind person and listened attentively whenever Frank spoke. Patty showed an interest in the things that concerned him. She was also attractive and had a witty charm. As Frank mused on all of Patty's wonderful qualities, his soul was ensnared in a trap.

Time passed and the couple's marital problems escalated. Frank and Shelia distanced themselves further and further from each other.

Shelia became involved with an online friend. She

embraced the refreshing spark of this new relationship. Her friend's name was Alex.

Alex seemed to listen attentively when Shelia discussed her problems and always offered her the sympathy she craved. And as Shelia began sharing her marital troubles with Alex, an unholy bond formed between the two of them. Shelia was oblivious to the fact that Belial had brought Alex into her life and that he was the bait to ensnare her soul.

One day Alex suggested they meet in person. He asked if Shelia would like to get a cup of coffee, and she eagerly agreed.

When Alex and Shelia met, they reminisced like old friends. The two talked, laughed, and enjoyed each other's company for hours.

Alex charmed Shelia for quite some time. At the right moment he persuaded her to go back to his place. When Alex and Shelia got to his house they indulged in physical sin. Shelia had fallen into Belial's trap.

While Shelia and Alex were together, Frank continued his quest to experience some new passion of his own. Frank found himself constantly daydreaming about a perfect companion, someone who would fit the illusion of what he desired in a woman. Frank wanted a woman who was kind, pleasant, attractive, and interested in him; he wanted someone like Patty.

As Patty loomed larger in his imagination, Frank surrendered to his impulses. He volunteered for extra work at the office, hoping this would enable him to spend more time with Patty. The strategy would prove to be a success.

One evening, while Frank and Patty were alone at work, something drew them together. They gazed into each other's eyes, igniting their desires. With his decision to indulge in a moment of passion, Frank had also become guilty of adultery.

Because they failed to exercise self-control, Frank and Shelia became victims of themselves and of Belial. Frank was full of guilt, and Shelia experienced enormous shame. They didn't try to cover up their actions, and decided to separate. Frank and Shelia had no idea the pain and suffering they were about to experience in their separate lives.

Patty told Frank she was pregnant with his child. Both were excited about the news until the miscarriage. After the baby's death, Patty suffered with depression. She became distraught and decided it was necessary to move as far away from Frank as possible. She had to move because every time her eyes looked at him she was reminded of the baby.

Frank became full of sorrow and regret because of the choices he had made. As pain and grief extinguished all the hope he had, Frank decided to take his own life.

Shelia continued dating Alex until she found out he was cheating on her. From that moment on, Shelia drifted from one bad relationship to another. She started losing control of her life and suffered the pain of loneliness.

Life became so unbearable for Shelia that she began

consuming large amounts of booze to help alleviate the pain. For three years, she would drink a fifth of hard liquor every night. Shelia eventually died prematurely of liver failure.

The rebel kingdom successfully claimed Frank and Shelia's eternal souls. They willingly submitted themselves to Belial's deceptive ploy and now experience torment for eternity. All this pain and suffering resulted from their decisions to enter into Belial's deadly realm of pornography.

Fraud

Fraud is prevalent in our society and has affected the lives of many people throughout time. This is another realm that Belial presides over for the rebel kingdom. From this realm the crown prince can impose pain, loss, and suffering on his victims in a variety of ways.

Fraud is particularly dangerous because it can take place just about anywhere. Even charitable ventures are not immune. Numerous groups say they want to help care for underprivileged children, provide for widows, feed the hungry, aid the sick, protect the weak, and assist the elderly. But do they?

Some of these programs do splendid work. They are feeding the less fortunate, clothing those who would otherwise be naked, and providing medical assistance to the sick. This is the intent of many who operate these humanitarian enterprises.

However, some people ask for charitable donations to line their own pockets. These people are not interested in helping others, just themselves. They appear sincere in public, but embezzle from the poor to live comfortable lives. People like this knowingly or unknowingly submit themselves to Belial by engaging in fraud.

The realm of fraud does not discriminate. Belial and his minions welcome all who are willing to enter this realm regardless of age, race, or gender. Many accept this invitation, as people all over the world commit fraudulent acts every day. And although these con artists may differ in appearance, they have one thing in common. Through their deceitful endeavors, they have become entangled with Belial.

GOD has spoken strongly against fraudulent acts and opposes those who commit them. The Holy Bible contains many warnings against fraud. One of those cautions can be found in the Old Testament book of Jeremiah 22:13. This verse tells what will happen to someone who gathers unjust gains. The verse reads as follows:

"Woe unto him that buildeth his house by unrighteousness, and his chambers by wrong; that useth his neighbor's service without wages, and giveth him not for his work;"

Notice the first word in this verse is *Woe*, which means sorrow. GOD warns people not to defraud one another or they will face the consequences: a curse of sorrow.

Belial is aware of what GOD said. However, he wants all those involved in a fraudulent scheme to suffer. The goal for the crown prince is to make sure everyone loses.

Belial puts the first stage of his diabolical plan in motion when he or a representative of his persuades someone to take something that does not belong to them. Initially, in any act of fraud, the targeted person or business suffers a loss. The items taken do not have to be large or valuable. In fact, small and inexpensive things can be obtained without raising a lot of suspicion.

Many examples can be cited. A store clerk might overcharge people at the checkout counter and pocket the extra cash when no one is watching. Employees may use company property for their own purposes, increasing business expenses. Service companies might unlawfully add to their customers' monthly bills, masking these fraudulent costs with words like *surcharges*.

Belial's plan is completed when the people who commit fraud lose. The perpetrators will lose because GOD said woe will come to those who gather unjust gain. GOD warned what will happen if people defraud one another, just as HE warned people they will reap what they sow.

The law of reciprocity is real, and anyone questioning this can ask a person like Mr. Bernie Madoff. Mr Madoff was sentenced to more than a century in prison for embezzling money from his clients. Not only did his clients lose their money and belongings, but Mr. Madoff lost the right to live as a free man. The only winners in any fraudulent transaction are Belial and the rebel kingdom.

The Fortress of Solitude

Lucifer assigned Belial to a key position in the rebel kingdom. This appointment established him as a crown prince and placed him over a vast array of demonic agencies. Though Belial has a variety of offices at his disposal, he governs from a designated primary headquarters. This headquarters is located deep within a hidden supernatural fortress of solitude. In the halls of this fortress, Belial legislates all manner of evil for the rebel kingdom.

To locate this fortress one must gaze into the second heaven, and look into a supernatural region around the earth's atmosphere. This area is positioned between the third realm of heaven and the plains of earth. In this territory Belial has permission to exercise his authority, which he uses to wage war against humanity.

Evidence regarding Belial's hidden fortress is found in the Holy Bible. An explanation of the rebel kingdom's dominion appears in the New Testament book of Ephesians 6:12. The verse reads as follows:

"For we wrestle not against flesh and blood, but against principalities, against powers, against the rulers of the darkness of this world, against spiritual wickedness in high places."

This verse offers valuable information, pointing out there are "rulers of the darkness of this world." Any earthly ruler or governing body of a kingdom is provided with a headquarters from which to reign. The rebel kingdom is no different with its fortress of solitude.

This verse also says there is "spiritual wickedness in high places." "Spiritual wickedness" can suggest the rebel kingdom's leaders, while "in high places" could point toward their whereabouts. The phrase "in high places" may refer to the second heaven.

Scripture presents irrefutable evidence by placing together the information that "the rulers of the darkness" have a main headquarters and that their "spiritual wickedness" is located "in high places." This information verifies that there is a fortress in the second heaven and that this fortress of solitude is occupied by Belial and the rebel kingdom.

CHAPTER 4

Belial's Power

Belial is a powerful being. His persuasive powers have entrapped people all over the world for centuries. He roamed the earth long before Adam and Eve, so this Archon was afforded opportunity after opportunity to observe and study mankind.

Based on his many observations, Belial has developed numerous effective techniques for penetrating the human soul.

One of these techniques depends upon obtaining knowledge of a deep-seated emotion within a person. The emotion can vary from pain and sorrow to joy and desire. Belial and his minions can use this technique as long as the emotion is deeply rooted within the target's soul.

Whatever the emotional vulnerability, once exposed to dark forces, the person will come under assault. The objective of this attack is to create a painful scenario with a destructive outcome for the victim. To illustrate how Belial and his forces implement this type of warfare, a few short stories are offered.

Natalie

Natalie was six years old when her dad walked away from the family. He cared for his wife and children, but his addiction to crack cocaine became more important to him.

Natalie loved her dad and did not understand what was happening. She use to spend every possible moment with him, but now he was no longer there. And as the days passed, this daddy's girl became confused.

Days turned into weeks, weeks turned into months, and months turned into years. Natalie still struggled with the pain of abandonment. Once full of energy and life, Natalie sat around and showed little enthusiasm for anything. Because of her dad's decisions, this little girl had been subjected to heart-wrenching sorrow.

Then, just when she thought things could not get any worse, Natalie suffered even more emotional pain. She became the target of verbal attacks by her older brother, John. He unknowingly repeated the hateful words whispered to him by Belial's invisible agents, telling Natalie, "You're the reason Dad left, and if it wasn't for you he would still be here."

These verbal assaults began to take hold of Natalie's thoughts. Then one day John's false accusations planted something deep within his sister's heart. For the first time, Natalie felt responsible for their dad's disappearance.

John's malicious words were harmful for other reasons. Since their father's departure, Natalie had leaned heavily upon her brother for guidance and comfort. She depended on John to be there for her, but then the verbal abuse started. The security this little girl once felt with her brother had now turned to anguish.

Eventually the pain brought on by her dad's desertion, combined with the emotional and mental wounds Natalie suffered in believing she was the reason her father left, began to reshape the little girl's thoughts. This had major consequences. As the years passed, Natalie began to experience extreme bouts of depression.

By the time Natalie turned fifteen, her psychological and emotional baggage was threatening to overwhelm her. Natalie knew that to free herself from this turmoil she needed to escape from her environment.

Not long after Natalie began to entertain these thoughts of freedom, she made a rash decision to leave her family. With scant preparation, this teenager ran away from home in the middle of the night.

Natalie had stashed a little cash and used some of it for a cab. She was on her way to a new life, heading for the home of someone she had met and befriended on a social media network. The new friend's name was Ella.

Posing as a traveling college student, Natalie had carried on many online conversations with Ella. She made it seem as if she were on break from her studies and was coming to town for a long vacation. One thing had led to another in their conversations, and out of the blue Ella, who lived alone, had offered to let Natalie stay with her. She wasted no time in accepting Ella's offer.

When Natalie arrived at Ella's, they acted as if they

were old friends. The two hit it off from the start, even though they were decades apart in age. But the relationship worked because Ella was looking for a friend to live with, and Natalie was looking for a new start away from her family and her past.

Ella had a nice home. She had plenty of room and gave Natalie the use of a private bedroom and bathroom. Ella told Natalie she could do odd jobs around the house and stay for free in return. The young girl quickly agreed.

The two enjoyed one another's company. Peace reigned in this home, and everything seemed to work out fine. But although her new environment was a dramatic change from what she had escaped, Natalie still struggled mentally and emotionally.

Ella noticed Natalie seemed sad and wanted to help her new friend but didn't know how. Then one evening she offered Natalie a glass of wine. Ella knew a little wine brought her some comfort and thought it might help Natalie as well. Unbeknown to Ella, Belial was using her in his plan for Natalie. The two shared the entire bottle, and by the end of the evening both were sound asleep.

In the days following her first experience with alcohol, Natalie continued to dwell on the minor relief she believed the beverage had brought her. How simple it was to drink something and to be temporarily relieved of stress and anxiety. It was easy for Natalie to convince herself that if booze helped her relax before, it could provide her the relaxation she needed again. Unknowingly Natalie continued to fall further into Belial's trap.

Given her mental and emotional state, this young girl was willing to try anything to numb her pain. Almost thoughtlessly Natalie chose to self-medicate and began to drink alcohol whenever she had an opportunity. She thought she might finally have found a way to cope with past agonies, but Natalie's life was starting to spin out of control.

Due to Natalie's deep feelings of abandonment and loneliness, she surrounded herself with others who indulged in liquid comfort. Consuming the amounts of alcohol she did intensified her hopelessness and depression. And with her growing addiction, Natalie was becoming more vulnerable to the wiles of Belial.

While Natalie drank it up with her growing circle of alcoholic friends, Belial began the next stage of his diabolical plan for her demise. The crown prince made arrangements for one of his followers to befriend Ella. The follower's name was Tommy.

One day Tommy found out Ella was giving a party at her home and invited himself. At the party Ella introduced Tommy to Natalie. The two immediately hit it off, becoming instant friends.

Natalie was excited about having Tommy for a friend. She began to think her life might turn around because Tommy seemed to like her.

As Natalie and Tommy spent more time together, the physical attraction between them grew. One day while they were drinking wine, Tommy enticed Natalie sexually.

Natalie believed she was in love and thought Tommy felt the same way.

Intoxicated, Natalie made a poor and distorted choice. She decided to surrender herself to Tommy. Natalie was willing to give everything she had to him, but Tommy kept a dark secret from his new lover: he was HIV positive.

After their sinful encounter, Natalie and Tommy could not stay away from each other. The two were inseparable at parties. Their dates always consisted of getting drunk and having sex.

Then Natalie began to feel a little sick in the morning. After two weeks of experiencing this morning sickness, she decided to see a doctor. So she made an appointment.

When she arrived at the doctor's office a nurse asked her some questions. The nurse then suggested Natalie take a pregnancy test. The test confirmed Natalie was pregnant.

She could not contain her excitement. Natalie was going to be a mom. The young teen could not wait to share the news with Tommy.

When Natalie returned to Ella's house, she called Tommy and asked him to come over. She told Tommy she had good news to share with him. He told her he was busy but would be there as soon as he could.

Tommy finally arrived and rang the doorbell. Natalie's excitement was evident when she opened the door. After giving him a big hug, she said, "I'm pregnant."

Tommy immediately recoiled from her embrace and looked at her in disbelief. Natalie stood stunned at his response. This human agent of Belial didn't say a word. Tommy simply turned around and walked away, never to be heard from again.

A wave of uncontrollable emotion overtook Natalie as feelings of abandonment and rejection resurfaced. Her father's desertion, her brother's abuse, and a host of other nightmarish memories flooded Natalie's mind. Once again she wondered what was wrong with her.

Time passed and Natalie found out that she was HIV positive and that her baby would be born with the killer virus. After receiving the horrible news, Natalie was completely overcome by guilt, fear, shame, and rage. With so much uncertainty and stress magnifying her feelings of hopelessness and doom, Natalie suffered a heart attack. She and her baby died three days before Natalie's sixteenth birthday.

What devastation this young girl experienced in her short life! Natalie's suffering began at a young age as a result of Belial's handiwork. The crown prince weakened Natalie and used other people to deepen her instability. In this vulnerable state, Natalie was pressured into making poor choices for herself. Belial used these poor decisions to bring about more pain and suffering and the premature death of Natalie and her unborn baby.

What a Buck Can Get

Belial and his regime have gained great power over people by encouraging materialism. The crown prince seeks to persuade people that money is everything. He promotes the idea that wealth and pleasure should be the focus of life.

There is nothing wrong with having money and possessions. However, prosperity should not be life's main objective.

Belial's promotion of materialism has done harm to many people. Here is a story about one of them.

Jim was a good man. He had a great job and worked very hard. This man did not want to be in debt and quickly paid for everything he purchased.

He began to put aside money to buy something special. Jim wanted to ask his girlfriend to marry him, and he needed an engagement ring. Jim loved Teresa but did not want to ask her to be his wife until he had a token of his affection to put on her finger.

Jim finally saved enough money for a beautiful ring. He called Teresa after he bought the ring and asked her to dinner. That night after they had finished eating, Jim stood up, got down on one knee in the restaurant, and popped the question.

Smiling from ear to ear, Teresa said yes. Jim and Teresa were officially engaged. Now they could begin planning the rest of their lives together.

The couple married, and a few months after their

honeymoon, the newlyweds learned they were going to have a child. Jim and Teresa were very excited, and they prepared for the baby's arrival.

One of their first priorities was to readjust their finances. They knew the baby would need quite a few things, and they began to shop for these items. Jim and Teresa quickly realized these necessities would not be cheap.

Months later the family grew to three as Teresa gave birth to a son, Steve.

It took Jim and Teresa time to adjust to having a newborn around. Life at home became so busy that Teresa was forced to quit her job. She hated to do it, but caring for Steve came first.

The couple now had to depend solely on Jim's income to support the family. Jim made enough for them to have what they needed as long as they stuck to a budget. And although there was not an abundance of money, Jim, Teresa, and Steve lived contentedly because everybody was healthy and happy and they had life's necessities.

Then when Steve turned eight months old, Teresa learned she was pregnant again. Months later Jamie and Stacy joined the family. With the family of three rapidly becoming a family of five, the couple now had far greater responsibilities than they originally planned.

Life quickly changed for Jim and Teresa as the demands made on them grew. Because they now have a large family, Jim and Teresa had to be even more frugal with time and resources.

While Teresa managed the home and was the

children's main caretaker, Jim worked every hour possible to provide the income his family needed. After work, Jim dashed home to help his wife care for the children and do household chores. It seemed that every dollar Jim made went to support their family and that every waking minute he and Teresa had was spent tending to their children and their home.

As the years passed and the daily grind continued, Jim and Teresa faced mounting stress. The two felt something had to change in their lives.

Then one night while Teresa was giving the children baths, something outside the kitchen window caught Jim's eye as he washed the dishes. Rick, their neighbor, had just returned home driving a new truck. This wasn't just any truck, though. It was the truck Jim had wanted for years but was unable to afford.

Jim stared at Rick's truck for what seemed like forever. Temptation overtook Jim, and he wished he could make that new truck his own. With Belial's subtle encouragement, Jim gave in to the sin of covetousness.

Through Jim's covetous desire, Belial was able to enter his life. With this one submission, the Archon had gained leverage over Jim.

Without hesitation, Belial attempted to influence his thinking. Jim began to hear little voices whispering in his ear, telling him how he had always been shortchanged.

This belief, combined with his new materialistic desires, caused Jim to wonder what might happen if he made some changes in his life. What if the way he raised and provided for his family changed? Should he continue to scrape by and take a hands-on approach to raising his children, or should he focus on making enough money to solve any issues the family might encounter?

While Jim pondered these questions (presented by Belial's agents), voices from the crown prince asked another question: Why couldn't he work more so he and his family would have more?

Jim fantasized about the luxuries he could have if only he worked more. Belial's agents reinforced these illusions, and Jim made a decision without consulting Teresa. He decided the money he earned was more important to his family than the time he spent at home.

Jim acted immediately to reposition his life. He volunteered for every work assignment available and began spending a lot more time on the job. Soon after his workload doubled, Jim started to receive the added money he desired.

But not everything was going well in his life. Jim's job started to consume all his time, and his work schedule created a strain between him and Teresa. Because he chose to work more, Jim could not help with the children and the household.

Months passed and Jim got the truck he wanted. Teresa hoped he would slow down, but she was sorely disappointed. He couldn't slow down because his buying obsession did not end with the truck. After obtaining it, Jim purchased one thing after another.

Jim was changing in front of his family's eyes. This

man had become obsessed with possessing all kinds of things. By now Jim was completely persuaded by Belial's agents that owning things would prove his success to his family and to the world.

To maintain his materialistic lifestyle, Jim went from working fifty hours a week to putting in eighty-plus hours. It appeared Jim did not mind these long hours because he always volunteered for new assignments. Jim had to work to preserve the status he had created for himself. Completely dedicated to materialism, he kept up this demanding schedule for the next twenty years.

Then one day a thought crossed his mind. He paused for a minute and took a deep breath. Jim began to question what he had gained with his years of hard work. What cost had he paid for accumulating the latest and greatest stuff?

Tears filled Jim's eyes as he realized that in his quest for prosperity, he had lost the thing once dear to him: his family. Jim trembled as he faced the truth. He had traded the sacred privilege of marriage and parenting for a luxurious lifestyle.

Jim suffered torment as he realized what he had sacrificed. Too late he saw that his children had needed his guidance while they were growing up but he hadn't been there. Now they had reached adulthood and knew him as a great gift-giver but not as a great mentor. He thought about the wife he had left to struggle with raising three children and maintaining a home by herself.

Jim finally saw that all his labor for this and that had been in vain. He felt agony knowing his family didn't need all the stuff he had worked so hard to accumulate. What his wife and children really needed was a husband and a dad who was there for them when it counted the most.

Who Is Vulnerable?

It should never be underestimated how vulnerable someone's home can become to Belial and his forces. The crown prince will make every effort to invade people's dwellings and to destroy their lives.

Many people do not realize that Belial is targeting their families. Shrouding himself in secrecy so his work will go unnoticed, the Archon attempts to introduce various forms of corruption into the environments of his targets.

Belial hopes that people will allow him to plant his poisonous notions in their minds. The crown prince understands that if someone accepts a corrupt thought, this thought will catch fire and consume the person's mentality.

Belial can inject his poisonous thoughts into human minds by many means. He is crafty at making temptations to greed, sensuality, and other forms of immorality seem appealing. The Archon and his forces can access a person's environment through television programs, radio broadcasts, newspapers, magazines, and the Internet.

Regardless of the access point Belial may use, his objective is the same. He wants to surround humanity with as much corruption as possible. To show how easily the crown prince can maneuver his way into someone's home, and the devastating effects of his presence once he is there, a short story is offered.

Bob and Sally were an average striving middle-class couple. Both had very busy schedules. They were self-made people who had goals and wanted to live a certain lifestyle. They had to labor long hours to maintain this lifestyle. Because the couple chose to work these hours, they surrendered many opportunities to spend quality time with their two little boys, Daniel and James.

While Bob and Sally worked, the boys were in school. When they left school, Daniel and James went to Grandma Ida's. Although Sally and Bob were sure their sons would be safe with Bob's mom, Belial's agents were pursuing a plan to destroy the boys' lives.

The rules Grandma Ida had for the boys were different from those at home. While at Grandma's, Daniel and James were permitted to watch as much television as they wanted. The boys would park themselves in front of the television in the living room as she viewed one in her bedroom. Grandma Ida didn't pay much attention to what they did.

Daniel was the older boy. He became the first of the brothers to be introduced to graphic television programs featuring cops and robbers. This little boy was only allowed to view violent and bloody shows at his grandmother's. So while Daniel's eyes were fixed on the screen at her home, Belial's agents took the opportunity to begin confusing his innocent mind.

Some of these shows impressed upon Daniel that the bad guys were really good guys and that the good guys were really bad guys. One day Daniel thought about that idea and paused for a minute. If this idea were so, it would be normal to hope the bad guys won. From that moment on, Daniel always pulled for the criminals.

Daniel was easily persuaded by certain shows instigated by Belial's forces. His little brother had noticed Daniel's growing obsession with these television programs because he watched his brother's every move and had seen parts of the shows himself.

Within a short time the younger boy's attitude shifted. Once independent, James began to behave differently. Now all he wanted to do was hang out with Daniel in front of the television. Daniel's actions were having an overwhelming influence on James. This was understandable because the boys spent more time with each other than with anyone else.

The brothers' relationship soon changed even further. When they were together, Daniel took the dominant role. He did this because he had been persuaded by Belial that he should be totally in charge. When he wanted to watch a particular television show or to play a certain game, James agreed without hesitation.

Belial's presence was obviously reshaping their lives. Daniel and James were changing. But the crown prince wasn't through yet.

As he grew older, Daniel's admiration for criminals increased. He adopted a tough-guy mentality. The young man became so caught up in criminal fantasies that he tried to take on the personas of his favorite television crime bosses. Little did Daniel realize this posturing would nurture a rebellious, hostile, and reckless attitude in his heart.

James was still the same. Without reservation, he went along with his brother and supported Daniel in every possible way. James looked up to Daniel because Daniel had always been there for him. James never became a fan of the criminal element, but he became a fan of Daniel.

When the boys were old enough to move away from home, Daniel wanted his independence and convinced James to join him in a new adventure of freedom.

As the brothers discussed where they should live, it became evident some things would not change. Daniel wanted to make the final decision, and James wound up submitting to his will. As always, he agreed to whatever Daniel wanted to do.

Daniel finally found an affordable apartment he liked. Shortly after the brothers settled into their new place, a covert operative of Belial introduced Daniel to a couple of shady characters named Nick and Donnie.

Once these three guys got to know each other better, Daniel found out Nick and Donnie shared his passion for crime. The trio's friendship grew quickly.

It seemed as if Nick and Donnie were always hanging out at Daniel's place. One day Daniel suggested they move in with him and James. It made sense to everyone that living expenses would be cheaper if they were divided four ways instead of two. Eventually Donnie and Nick moved in with Daniel and James.

Not long after that, spirits sent by Belial aided Daniel in designing a sinister plan. Daniel suggested to his roommates that a life of crime would be an easy ticket to good living.

Nick and Donnie quickly agreed. At first James was a little reluctant. Later he acted somewhat interested because Daniel had suggested the idea. Even in his adult years James was willing to do anything for his older brother.

Daniel suggested the four of them rob a bank. He knew a small bank that had only one security guard. Supposedly it would be filled with enough money for them to start a new life somewhere else. Nick and Donnie jumped at the chance. After a few minutes, James agreed to join Daniel on the heist.

The would-be robbers went to work. One week later Daniel, Nick, and Donnie finalized plans to rob the bank. That same week James had been forced to go with the other three to steal the guns they needed to pull off the heist.

On the day of the robbery, Belial directed Daniel to change the target. Instead of robbing the small bank as planned, the gang targeted an armored truck that pulled up outside the bank. Daniel was led to believe the truck would be an easier target and full of money.

Two security guards exited the truck and headed for the bank. Daniel and his crew were in position to make their strike. Suddenly, the two guards found themselves surrounded by four armed men in masks.

Then, to the criminals' surprise, two more security guards appeared out of nowhere. Now it was four against four.

After a brief standoff, Nick pulled the trigger on his gun. Both the guards and the bandits took cover and began exchanging fire.

Within minutes of the first shot, police cars arrived on the scene. Daniel and his gang quickly surrendered after realizing they were surrounded and outnumbered. As officers subdued him to the ground for handcuffing, Daniel was stunned by what he saw to his right.

One of his masked accomplices lay motionless on the ground. His chest had been blown wide open during the gunfight. A police officer walked over to the lifeless body and removed the mask. Daniel's shock turned to horror as he gazed upon the face of his brother James.

Daniel was immediately overcome with emotion. He trembled and sobbed as guilt overtook him. Daniel realized he was ultimately responsible for his brother's death. He would have to live with that knowledge for the rest of his life.

Daniel did not know he and his brother had been left vulnerable to this fate at an early age. As children, they were permitted to sit in front of the television unsupervised and faced the persuasive tactics of Belial alone.

Judas

Belial's persuasive tactics have brought pain, suffering, and death to countless generations. Strong and agile, he continues to operate in today's society through targeting people from all walks of life.

Even Jesus encountered Belial's influence during His earthly ministry, though not as some would think. When Jesus dwelled in the flesh on earth two thousand years ago, He was tempted to sin just like every human being. Jesus, however, never surrendered to the tactics of the dark kingdom. He in no way attached Himself to the workings of Belial.

However, a man whom Jesus befriended would become Belial's inside man among Christ's disciples. This man was Judas Iscariot.

The name Judas Iscariot has been notorious throughout history. Jesus chose Judas and eleven other men to be His disciples. These men were taught and trained by Jesus Himself. Each disciple was assigned a position in the Lord's ministry, because every man must learn to serve. Judas became the ministry accountant. He was selected to be the person responsible for overseeing the ministry's finances.

Although in training to be a disciple of Christ, Judas was different from the rest of the ministry team. Judas had become a thief. He embezzled funds from the ministry.

Proof of Judas's crimes can be found in GOD'S Word.

The charge is verified in the New Testament book of John 12:4–6. This passage reads as follows:

4. Then saith one of his disciples, Judas Iscariot, Simon's son, which should betray him,

5. Why was not this ointment sold for three hundred pence, and given to the poor?

6. This he said, not that he cared for the poor; but because he was a thief, and had the bag, and bare what was put therein.

These verses prove Judas was misappropriating funds. Verse 5 shows Judas attempting to conceal his true goal under the guise of a charitable act. He asks why the precious ointment couldn't be sold and the proceeds given to the poor. This sounds like a noble idea, but what was Judas's real intent?

Verse 6 eliminates any doubt. Judas did not care about the needy. Any money the ministry received would fall under his control. And if the ministry had more money, he could easily acquire a portion without being noticed.

Verse 6 plainly states Judas "was a thief." This proves his true motive. This verse confirms Judas was capable of scheming to get his hands on money. But embezzlement would be just the beginning for this wayward disciple of Christ.

Belial and his minions set many traps that brought Judas into sin, but their plot did not stop with that. The kingdom of darkness had far more important assignments for Judas. These assignments were designed to have a greater impact on Jesus' ministry.

Because he became caught up in thievery, Judas probably continued to take every opportunity to skim money from the ministry. Judas may have believed his embezzlement would not be detected, but he was mistaken. Belial knew every time Judas helped himself to ministry money. And while manipulating Judas through greed, Belial set the stage for the next phase of his evil plan.

Various minions suggested a troubling possibility to Judas. They wanted him to believe that because he was taking so much money, someone would soon discover his embezzlement.

As the possibility of being exposed began to consume Judas, Belial easily introduced additional ideas into the subconscious of this fretting man. One suggestion was that Judas swindle the money he needed. So Judas tried to think of any wealthy people he knew.

Invisible agents of the crown prince quickly pointed out to Judas that many wealthy people had tried to discredit or sabotage Jesus but had failed because the Creator was with Him.

Judas realized Jesus was invincible, but Belial's agents presented the disciple with a proposition. What if there were a way for Judas to profit by orchestrating a confrontation between Jesus and a wealthy opponent? (It wasn't hard to convince Judas that Jesus could handle any clash, because he had seen the Lord do it every time.) And what if Judas made enough money from this endeavor to pay back what he had stolen from the ministry? With the missing money repaid, no one would ever learn that Judas had stolen the funds.

Because he was desperate, Judas considered this scam despite the risk. He knew any plot in which he involved Jesus was a big gamble, but Belial assured Judas that the gamble would pay off and that he would then be out of trouble.

Judas still had to choose a target for this charade. Then Belial cleverly reminded him that the temple priests were rich and had always had it in for Jesus. They were also easily and inconspicuously accessible.

So Judas decided to approach the priests. When the opportunity presented itself, he secretly made an arrangement to betray the Christ for money.

GOD'S Word verifies the backroom deal Judas made with the temple priests. This shady business transaction is recounted in the New Testament book of Matthew 26:14–16. This passage reads as follows:

14. Then one of the twelve, called Judas Iscariot, went unto the chief priest,

15. And said unto them, What will ye give me, and I will deliver him unto you? And they covenanted with him for thirty pieces of silver.

16. And from that time he sought opportunity to betray him.

Judas made a deal with the enemies of Jesus for thirty pieces of silver. It seemed Judas's troubles would soon be over. However, he still needed to do one thing to keep up his part of the bargain. Judas had to wait for the right moment and then lead the temple authorities to Jesus.

Judas may have believed that when the temple authorities showed up, Jesus would vanish as He had done so many times before. Judas may have thought it would be easy for Jesus to escape an angry mob, especially since His life would be at stake. And as long as Judas did everything he was supposed to do, but the temple guards allowed Jesus to escape, the priests could not withhold Judas's compensation. How could they when he had fulfilled his part of the bargain?

When the time was right, Judas led a mob to where he knew Jesus would be praying. The mob surrounded Jesus, but He showed no fear. Jesus went off with the guards because He knew it was time to complete His mission on earth. Jesus knew He needed to lay down His life so humanity could be free from the penalties of sin and from the bondages of Belial.

Judas probably stood speechless. Things had not gone according to his plan. Jesus had not escaped from the temple guards. The reality of Belial's deception quickly became evident.

The ideal situation he had hoped for turned into agony

and torment for Judas. He had become a traitor to the Christ. Now Judas, a man who had once walked with Jesus, had become an accomplice to what would soon be His murder.

However, Belial's agents were not finished with the faithless disciple. The Holy Bible shows what Belial had in store for Judas now that his services were no longer needed. Matthew 27:3–5 reveals the judgment Judas faced because of his sin. This passage reads as follows:

3. Then Judas, which had betrayed him, when he saw that he was condemned, repented himself, and brought again the thirty pieces of silver to the chief priest and elders,

4. Saying, I have sinned in that I have betrayed the innocent blood. And they said, What is that to us? see thou to that.

5. And he cast down the pieces of silver in the temple, and departed, and went and hanged himself.

Belial seemingly targeted two people but succeeded in getting only one. Jesus did not go to the cross because Belial and the agents of darkness forced Him to. Jesus went to the cross because He submitted Himself to the will of GOD, the Father of all creation.

While Jesus submitted Himself to GOD'S will, Judas chose to submit himself to the kingdom of darkness. Judas decided to steal from Jesus' ministry and willingly surrendered to the persuasive tactics of Belial. Judas then orchestrated a plan to betray Jesus. And because he had become completely entangled in deception, Judas finally hanged himself. He traded all the peace and power he could have received from Jesus and in return received destruction from Belial and the rebel kingdom.

CHAPTER 5

Other Names for Belial

Since the era of Adam and Eve, Belial has effectively concealed himself from most of humanity. Evolving through time, the crown prince has influenced many cultures and traditions.

Operating in personal anonymity, Belial has cleverly used an array of fictitious names to spread many false and deadly doctrines. His deceptions have influenced many creeds and generations, and have woven illusions before everyone from the pharaohs of Egypt to Queen Elizabeth I of England.

Alternative Names

One way Belial cloaks himself is through alternative names. But before beginning an investigation into these names, a warning must be offered. In this chapter certain illustrations from occult-themed materials will be referenced.

These materials are not recommended for reading or study. Occultism is demonically influenced and is designed to be cunning, alluring, and deceiving. Occult books, objects, or propaganda can carry an array of curses. These cursed items may have wicked spirits attached or assigned to them. If you have occult items in your home, you would be wise to dispose of them for your safety and for the safety of others.

Belial has inserted himself into human affairs by many deceptive means. One such deception occurred in the sixteenth century. This account begins with two men: Dr. John Dee and Mr. Edward Kelly.

Dr. Dee was born in 1527. He became an occultist and gained notoriety as an astrologer who served England's Queen Elizabeth I. Mr. Kelly was born in 1555. This man reportedly thought of himself as a person with vast magical abilities.

During occult rituals Dr. Dee and Mr. Kelly performed together, an extraordinary supernatural event supposedly took place. It was rumored that an extraterrestrial intelligence appeared and gave these two men a mystical alphabet written in an unknown language.

Dr. Dee and Mr. Kelly were also apparently given instructions on how to use this alphabet to operate magical systems. If properly executed, these systems could, among other things, be used to initiate supernatural gateways.

By accurately initiating these mysterious gateways, an individual would be placed in a position to summon or contact alien beings. If an alien life force responded to the human petition, a portal would be established between two realms. This act is an aspect of witchcraft known as Enochian magic.

This occult art centers around the alphabet system Dr. Dee and Mr. Kelly received from the rebel kingdom. Placed within this mystical dialect is a vast number of demonic leaders' names along with their hierarchy status.

At the top of the Enochian hierarchy are four names. Each is masked supposedly to represent the names of GOD. However, these names do not represent GOD the Creator. They are intended as alternate names for leaders in the rebel kingdom.

Elements are a clue connecting the Enochian names to the rebel leadership. Each of the four Enochian names for Creator has an element assigned to it. Comparing this information with material covered in chapter 3 clearly reveals the similarities. In both instances the same elements are identified with each main leader in the rebel kingdom.

The Enochian name for Belial deciphered from the mystical dialect is Mor-Dial-Hectega. This unique name can be pronounced Mor-Di-L-Hec-t-Gah.

There are many speculative interpretations of the name's meaning. Some Enochian translations deem the figure who bears this name to be one who is consumed with iniquity. Other Enochian translations identify Mor-Dial-Hectega as one who creates confusion and frustration to bring about personal gain and alliances. These interpretations describe Belial perfectly.

To further compare these interpretations of

Mor-Dial-Hectega to Belial, let's briefly refer back to chapter 1, which explained that Belial was consumed with wickedness (or iniquity) from the beginning. Chapter 1 showed Belial using his crafty arts to bring about confusion, frustration, and division. Then he used those same abilities to rally disillusioned creatures for a single purpose: to rebel against GOD. Chapter 1 also revealed Belial's drive for personal gain.

Considering the clues and interpretations regarding this name, along with the information from chapters 1 and 3, only one conclusion can be drawn: the name Mor-Dial-Hectega accurately describes Belial, his abilities, and his operating style.

The Earth God

Another name Belial has used to disguise himself can be traced back to the Middle East, notably in the period from 2600 BC to AD 400. During this time a certain deity was introduced into society through Egyptian folklore and religion. The deity's name was Geb.

Belial promoted the ideology of Geb to position himself to enter the lives of people rich or poor, slave or free. And as Geb became widely accepted and worshipped by the masses, Belial basked in their praise through one of his alternative names.

By way of Egyptian religious doctrines, many people in the time period were lured into believing the deity

Geb had created the earth's surface with its life-giving vegetation. Not only was Geb (sometimes pronounced Seb or Keb) credited with creating the earth's lush surface, but he received praise for being the deity responsible for the regeneration of the earth's vegetation. By propagating these beliefs, Belial deceived many into thinking he was responsible for the creation and regeneration of the life-giving substances earth produced.

These demonically influenced ideologies should be regarded as nothing more than clever schemes orchestrated from the pits of hell. The facts are the facts. It is a proven fact that GOD formed the earth's surface and everything on it.

Proof of this can be found in numerous places in the Holy Bible. Two examples are quickly located in the Old Testament book of Genesis, 1:1 and 1:9–12. These two passages read as follows:

1. **In the beginning God created the heaven and the earth.**

9. **And God said, Let the waters under the heaven be gathered together unto one place, and let the dry land appear: and it was so.**

10. **And God called the dry land Earth; and the gathering together of the waters called he Seas: and God saw that it was good.**

11. **And God said, Let the earth bring forth grass, the herb yielding seed, and the fruit tree yielding fruit after his kind, whose seed is in itself, upon the earth: and it was so.**

12. **And the earth brought forth grass, and herb yielding seed after his kind, and the tree yielding fruit, whose seed was in itself, after his kind: and God saw that it was good.**

These verses present overwhelming evidence proving GOD created the planet's land and vegetation. They also prove GOD was the one who ordained the regeneration and reproduction process for earth's life-giving substances.

When Belial tried to fashion himself into the image of a deity, he was attempting to deceive people into believing lies. Belial is no creator. In reality, he himself was created by GOD and formed in the image of the species known as the Archons.

Who's the Boss?

Belial has been assigned to an office in the rebel kingdom. He is seated at a high position in a monarchy. Due to his position within a ruling structure, Belial is referred to and addressed by various titles.

Although he retains many titles, only the title crown

prince will be reviewed because its intent and meaning are very important.

The title denotes a position of tremendous power in the rebel kingdom, and that authority is not taken lightly. The two words of the title together create a public declaration of authority.

The first word, *crown*, symbolizes sovereignty. When Lucifer refers to his three appointees with a title beginning with the word *crown*, he makes a statement about his reign, proclaiming he's sovereign king. So this word in essence demonstrates the supremacy of the dark king Lucifer.

The second part of the name, *prince*, refers to a rank or position. The title prince decrees that full acknowledgment and absolute obedience be given by all those in the rebel kingdom—all except Lucifer. He obeys no one in darkness but has established who will be responsible for governing portions of the dark kingdom for the fallen angel in his absence.

Placing these two words together, it is quite clear what Lucifer means by the title crown prince. With this title, Lucifer declares he is the supreme being in the rebel kingdom. This name informs those in Lucifer's kingdom of two important things. One, he has given a proxy status to those who bear the title of crown prince. Two, his followers must obey his proxies' commands as they would obey him.

This is how Belial can control a large population in the rebel kingdom. He wields power because he received Lucifer's seal of authority through the title crown prince.

Descriptive Names

Belial's presence can be recognized through descriptive names. In general, these are not given names or surnames but names derived from areas of someone's life.

One example would involve a girl who grows up and goes to college. This young lady then becomes a doctor who marries and has children. The woman's parents know her as their daughter, while her patients know her as doctor. Her husband calls her sweetie, and her kids call her mom. She is still the same person, although known by different names that describe particular areas of her life. Belial is no different. This is evident in some of his descriptive names.

The name Belial rarely surfaces in the media or in everyday life. The Archon likes keeping a low profile so he can be more effective in his mission to corrupt humanity. But while the name Belial is not widely publicized, the crown prince can appear under a multitude of aliases.

Provided for your convenience is a list of descriptive names and character traits for Belial, accompanied by biblical references. This list not only describes aspects of the Archon but includes important clues as to what Belial's presence may entail. This chart contains descriptive names some people may classify as offensive. These names, however, must be used to expose Belial.

Descriptive Names and Character Traits For Belial

1. Lover of Money   1 Timothy 6:7-11

2. Enemy of GOD   James 4:4
3. Drunkard   1 Samuel 1:13-16
4. Rapist   Genesis 34:2
5. Corruptor   II Peter 2:19

These five names not only describe some of Belial's core values but also reveal the vileness surrounding him. These names clearly identify the immorality and the crimes he instigates. Although all five names have vital meanings, only one will be covered.

Belial is ecstatic over what money can gain for him. Money is an effective tool to use in enslaving many humans for the rebel kingdom. But before Belial can enslave anyone, he must set a trap. Some of the most successful enticements Belial uses to capture people come from the financial arena.

GOD'S Word confirms the unbalanced love of temporal things is harmful to a person's life. One warning is found in the New Testament book of 1 Timothy 6:9–10. This passage reads as follows:

9. But they that will be rich fall into temptation and a snare, and into many foolish and hurtful lusts, which drown men in destruction and perdition.

10. For the love of money is the root of all evil: which while some coveted after, they have erred from the faith, and pierced themselves through with many sorrows.

These two verses provide important insights. Verse 9 proves there is a force looking to set traps, or a "temptation and a snare" to destroy people. This verse also explains the purpose of the traps, to "drown men in destruction and perdition."

Verse 10 points out "the love of money is the root of all evil." Belial is a being who is all evil. Because he operates a financially powerful global organization, the Archon has massive amounts of leverage and cleverly uses it to convince multitudes of people to pierce "themselves through with many sorrows."

This lover of money is very effective with his allurements and will bargain to acquire someone's soul. A soul consists of someone's mind (the way the person thinks), someone's will (what the person decides to do), and someone's emotions (how the person feels and relates). Once the crown prince has made his purchase, he waits until the day of death to claim his prize, an eternal soul.

Defeated

One final name will be mentioned for Belial: defeated. However, not everyone will address the crown prince by this name.

It is possible for Belial to be called defeated. But anyone who wants to call him this must act. The next chapter will show how it is possible for someone to call this powerful crown prince defeated.

CHAPTER 6

Belial: A Defeated Foe

Given all the information presented in chapters 1 to 5, it is understandable why Belial should be considered a supernatural entity to reckon with. Many examples have been offered to prove this.

Chapter 1 revealed how Belial's clever persuasiveness assisted Lucifer in deceiving and corrupting cosmic inhabitants and in turning them against GOD. Chapter 2 looked into GOD'S Word for information concerning the Archon. Then chapters 3 through 5 revealed a vast array of realms, powers, and names this crown prince has used throughout time. But although he's accumulated power and resources, one fact remains: Belial is not invincible.

In this final chapter, two examples of how Belial has tasted defeat will be offered. Two conclusions of stories from chapters 3 and 4 will be presented next. Finally, it will be demonstrated how people can defeat this crown prince—no matter who they are or what they have done.

So whether you are an interested reader who merely wants to finish the book, or know of someone possibly ensnared by Belial and his agents, or are yourself under an attack, please read on to see how Belial is defeated.

Belial's First Defeat

Although Belial retains massive capabilities, there was a time when he displayed only weakness. The Archon and his rebellious forces tried to subdue the celestial city but were quickly overtaken and beaten. In GOD'S city this crown prince first hung his head in utter defeat and was originally judged by the Almighty.

GOD then began to execute HIS judgments. The Almighty had Belial thrown from the third heaven and imprisoned within earth's atmosphere. The Archon's imprisonment continues here today. Belial's confinement is a demonstration he is a defeated foe.

Another Defeat

The crown prince experienced a major defeat when Jesus hung on the cross at Calvary and shed His precious blood. This event left Belial speechless.

When the Son of GOD hung on the cross, He provided full payment for humanity's sin debt. This huge sacrifice had to be made for one reason. Only the power of the blood of Jesus could cover and exercise complete authority over something as destructive as sin. The Lord's blood is the only substance able to redeem all the sinful acts of every person from Adam and Eve to the last individual who will be born during the age of grace in which we now live.

Again, GOD defeated Belial's attempt to overthrow HIS rule of order. The Almighty defeated the Archon in the heavens and then made a way to strip him of any authority he stole here on earth.

Surely it is easy to comprehend that GOD is all-powerful and has the authority to deal with this Archon. It is also certain that the power in the blood of Jesus is greater than sin. But what about us? What about the authority humanity should have when it comes to defeating this crown prince?

Is there something we as people can do to defeat our enemy? Is there something within us powerful enough to overcome Belial? Before answering these questions, let's revisit a couple of stories from previous chapters.

Turned Around: The Story Continues

In chapter 3 a short story was offered revealing Belial's realm of pornography. A man named Frank and his wife, Shelia, fell victim to Belial's tactics and ultimately perished. Through a surrender to passion and a moment of sin, a young lady named Patty became caught up in the scenario Belial cleverly orchestrated.

Patty distanced herself from Frank. Moving on from

their sordid affair became a priority for her. Patty knew she must leave behind the chaos that had become her world if she was going to survive.

But the ache deep in her heart didn't seem to go away. Patty's thoughts always returned to the miscarriage of her child. She wanted to heal emotionally, but Belial had other ideas. Through her pain, the crown prince felt confident he would eventually have her, just as he did Frank and Shelia.

Patty relocated to another town and quickly settled into a regular routine. Life became busy with a new job. While Patty attempted to rebuild her life, Belial's agents formulated plans for her demise.

One day something began to stir in this young lady's heart. The feeling would not go away. It tugged at Patty enough to cause her to make a decision.

A coworker had invited Patty to attend a support group, and she decided to go. After the first meeting, Patty thought this group might be beneficial for her, so she began to attend regularly.

Then one evening at a group meeting something special happened. As the opening prayer began, GOD'S presence filled the room.

After the prayer, Patty spoke up and asked something out of the blue. She had observed how these people seemed so loving, thoughtful, and caring toward everyone. Patty wanted to know what enabled them to be so gentle yet strong, especially after going through the heart-shattering events they discussed.

All those at the meeting said they were Christians. (Unbeknown to Patty or to Belial's agents, these people had been praying for Patty during their private prayer times.) Curious, Patty asked about Christianity and what it was.

People took turns offering their views on Christianity. Patty listened attentively to each one. As they shared testimonies, a deep longing grew in her soul. She wanted what everyone else had, and said so.

Patty prayed a sincere prayer and accepted Jesus as her Lord. At that second, angels shouted for joy while demonic forces gnashed their teeth. This lady had received forgiveness of her sins and eternal life from GOD.

Suddenly Patty began to weep. Out came the tears of pain and sorrow over a scarred relationship with a married man whom Belial used to seduce her. Out came the tears of rage and frustration. Out came the tears of hurt and betrayal. And out came the tears for her unborn infant.

From that moment on, Patty's life changed. Immediately her name was written in GOD'S Book of Life, and now she will live in HIS presence forever. Day by day, Jesus filled Patty's heart with joy and love and empowered her with confidence and truth. And with all she received, she gained the power to defeat Belial.

Another Chance

The second story comes from chapter 4. Daniel and James were once two little boys who were left at the mercy of Belial through the persuasive power of television. Twenty years later, because of bad choices and misguided ideas, Daniel was in prison while his brother's body lay cold in a grave.

Daniel received a long prison sentence but not for the robbery attempt alone. During the gun battle, he had shot and wounded a security guard. Daniel didn't mean to harm the man, but that's what he had done.

Guilt over his crimes and over his brother's death weighed heavily on Daniel. Belial's agents relentlessly bombarded this young man's thoughts with reminders of these events. Their fiendish goal was to push Daniel over the edge and grasp his eternal soul.

Then one day rumors began to circulate around the prison. The rumors turned into news that a ministry team would be visiting soon. This team had never been to the prison before, but the visit promised to be something out of the ordinary. All prisoners could attend as long as they were not in special confinement.

When the day arrived, the minister and his team showed up early. There wasn't a large crowd at first, but prisoners kept trickling in. They came for different reasons. Eventually there was standing room only.

Daniel was there because he had volunteered to work on a detail assigned to set up the event. He did this only because this helped him get out of a more unpleasant assignment. Belial's agents weren't concerned that Daniel was working this detail, because they thought they had him locked up.

The worship team took the makeshift stage and began to sing praises to GOD. The presence of the Most High could be felt all over the hall. By the time the evangelist ended his sermon there were tears in quite a few eyes. As the man of GOD gave an altar call, some of the inmates came forward to receive Christ as their Savior. Daniel was one of them.

Throughout this event the Spirit of GOD moved upon Daniel and allowed him to understand the issues he faced. For the first time in quite a while, Daniel had hope and purpose because he now had eternal life through Christ Jesus.

During the rest of his time behind bars, Daniel dedicated his life to serving GOD. He set an example, bringing others the good news of salvation through Christ. And he never forgot his brother James.

Daniel eventually was released to society. When Daniel went home to heaven, he left on earth a loving wife and three grown children. The oldest was named James.

As Daniel stood before GOD and witnessed all he had done on earth, he saw that hundreds of people may have been saved through his efforts. Daniel wept tears of joy. Then, to his surprise, he was reunited with James. Yes, his brother was also in heaven.

James was there because on the day he lay bleeding

from his chest, he remembered that someone had once told him about GOD and about a man named Jesus. So before James took his last breath, he sincerely asked GOD to forgive him of all his sins and cried out to Jesus.

How Can Anyone Defeat Belial?

Now what about those questions posed earlier in the chapter? What about humanity? Where do we gain authority over this crown prince? Is there something people can do to defeat Belial?

GOD loves humanity so much that HE made a way to redeem our sins and to give us all the authority we need over Belial if we want it. From cover to cover, the Holy Bible confirms GOD'S love for humanity. One example is found in the New Testament book of John 3:16. The verse reads as follows:

"For God so loved the world, that he gave his only begotten Son, that whosoever believeth in him should not perish, but have everlasting life."

This one verse sums up what GOD thought about humanity. This statement proves what HE was willing to sacrifice to give people a chance to save their eternal souls. GOD did HIS part in the redemptive process. Many people live defeated lives and eventually perish because they fail to activate and to operate by GOD'S protocol.

The authority from GOD to defeat Belial is easily available to people after they have accomplished two things. First, they must ask GOD for forgiveness of their sins by the precious blood of Jesus. Second, they must accept Jesus as the Son of GOD and make Him Lord of their lives.

Through these practical acts of faith, GOD pardons past transgressions and begins to restore and empower the person's life. This process is so important that a sample prayer has been provided. This prayer can guide anyone who is sincere about gaining GOD-given authority and eternal life through Christ Jesus. This prayer is just an example. Feel free to pray in your own words.

A Sample Prayer

Father, in the name of Jesus, I ask You to forgive me of all my sins. I confess that I am a sinner and need Your help. Your Word says in John 3:16 that You so loved the world that You gave Your only begotten Son, Jesus, that whosoever believes in Him should not perish but have everlasting life. Right now, by my free will, I believe that Jesus died for me and shed His blood for my sins. I choose to accept what He did for me and make Jesus Lord of my life. Help me to live a life pleasing to You. Thank You for saving me. In Jesus name I pray. Amen.

If you chose to pray this prayer or a prayer like it to GOD, believing it in your heart, you have become a child of the Most High. You have also become a brother or a sister to everyone in Christ; so welcome to the family. May our heavenly Father in Christ Jesus bless you and guide you along your new journey in life, ever directing you toward fulfillment in HIM.

People must make their own decisions and deal with the consequences. One question should be paramount. Can any human being justify his or her sins to a holy GOD on the day of judgment?

So not to pray this prayer, or never to have prayed a similar prayer in the past (confessing Jesus as Lord and Savior), eliminates the possibility of receiving GOD'S forgiveness for sins and trespasses. If a person's life past the age of accountability ends without GOD'S forgiveness of sins, this life will transition to a place of eternal separation and judgment. But this place is not abounding in sex, drugs, and rock and roll as many have been deceived into believing. On the contrary, this spiritual prison is full of pain, suffering, and the never-ending torture of recurring death.

This place of judgment was originally designed for Lucifer, Belial, and the rebel army of darkness, not for humanity. Things changed when Adam and Eve sinned. It was never GOD'S intent to send people to this dreadful place, and it is not HIS intent today.

GOD does not choose to send people to hell. People choose to send themselves to eternal damnation by refusing to accept what GOD provided to overcome the penalties of sin: the sacrifice of Jesus. GOD respects a person's free will. HE will allow each person to make his or her own choice, even if refusing the way of Jesus is accepting Belial's way. Remember, Belial's way is a way of defeat, a way of imprisonment, and a way to utter death.

Parting Words

Time is very precious and valuable, so thank you for taking the time to read volume four of *The Leadership Series: Heads of War*. This book was created to inspire, educate, and empower every person who may read it. If this book has been beneficial to you or to someone you know, kindly write or email info@hendertree.com to let me know. Your feedback is greatly appreciated.

So until the next time we explore another volume in *The Leadership Series* together, may GOD bless you, and may HE keep you safe in HIS arms.

For what is a man profited, if he shall gain the whole world, and lose his own soul ? or what shall a man give in exchange for his soul ?

Matthew 16: 26

Printed in the United States
By Bookmasters